LICENSE TO DREAM
A ROSE IS ROSE COLLECTION BY PAT BRADY

**Andrews McMeel
Publishing**

Kansas City

TO WATCH PASQUALE FLY PAST THE MOON, FAN THE PAGES WITH YOUR LEFT THUMB!

Read *Rose Is Rose* in your local newspaper
and on the World Wide Web:
www.unitedmedia.com

Send Pat Brady e-mail at: PBRADYROSE@AOL.COM

Send Pat Brady paper mail at:
Pat Brady (Rose Is Rose)
United Media
200 Madison Ave.
New York, NY 10016

TO SEE PASQUALE FLY THROUGH THE ROOF, FAN THE PAGES WITH YOUR RIGHT THUMB!

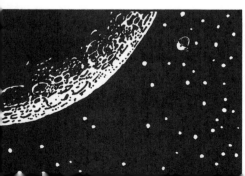

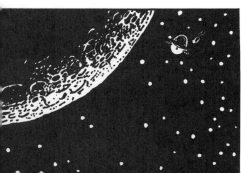

8

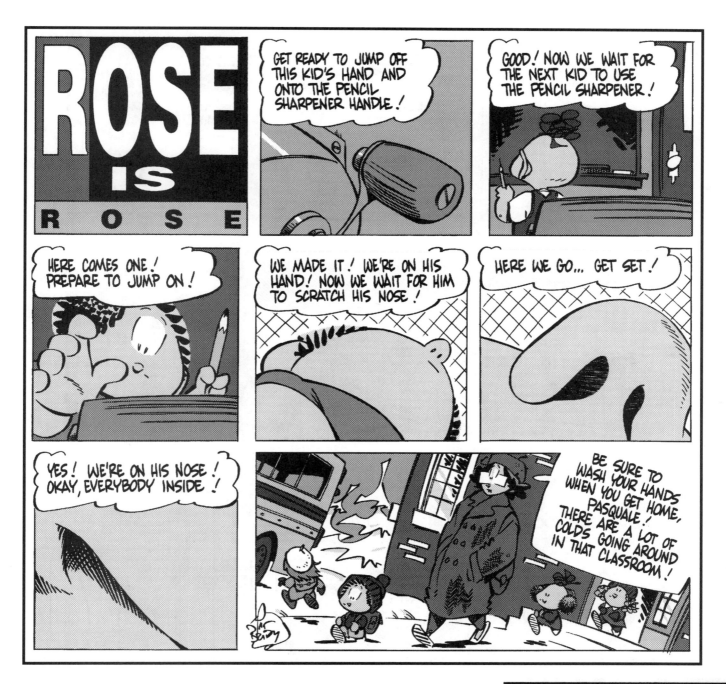

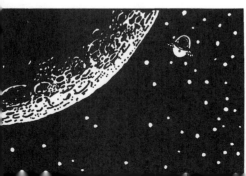

14

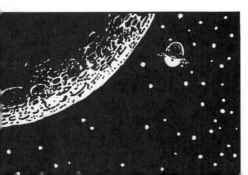

16

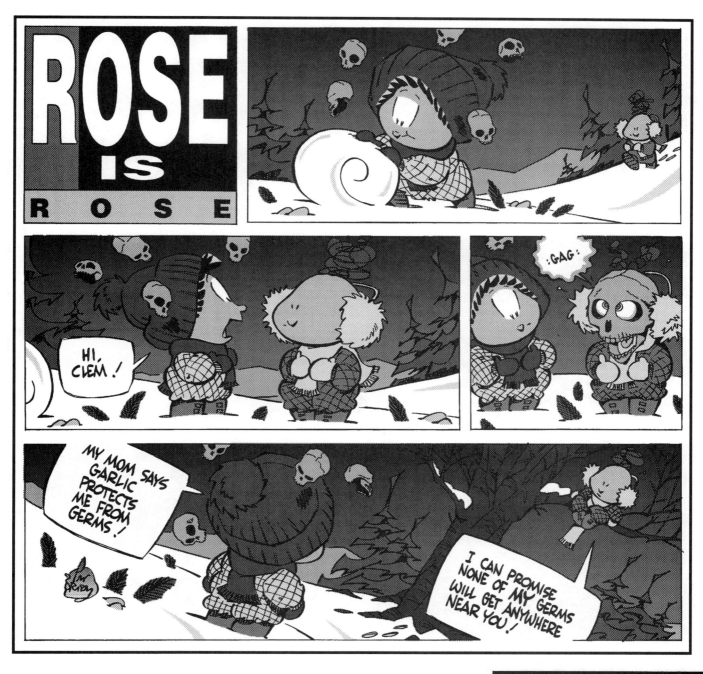

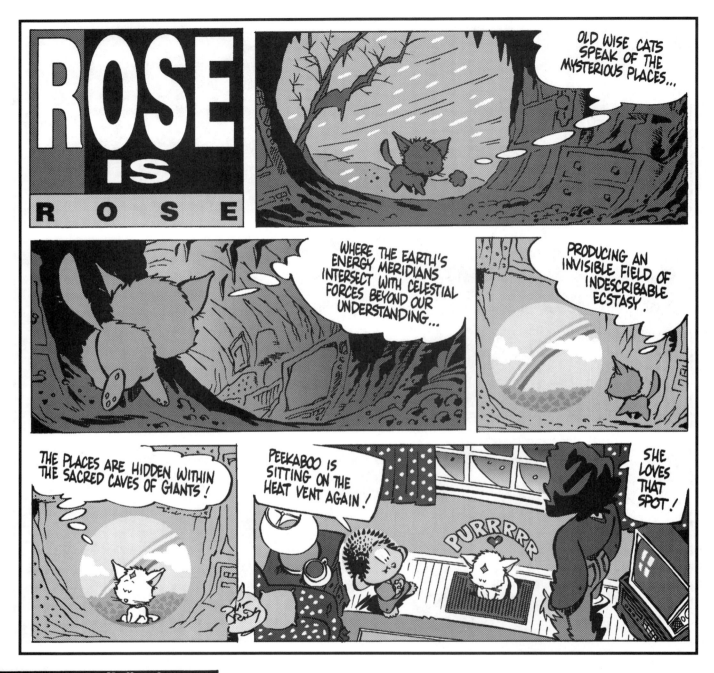

21

TO WATCH PASQUALE FLY PAST THE MOON, FAN THE PAGES WITH YOUR LEFT THUMB!

TO SEE PASQUALE FLY THROUGH THE ROOF, FAN THE PAGES WITH YOUR RIGHT THUMB!

27

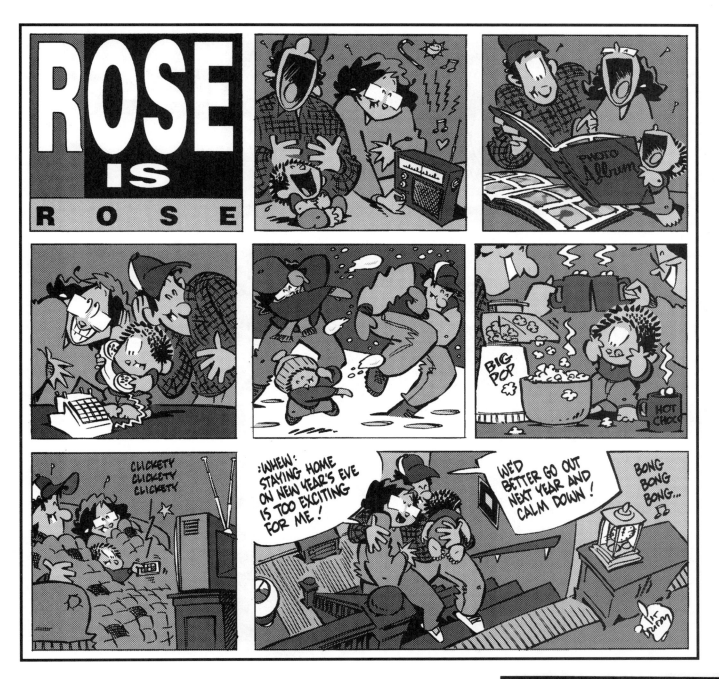

30

Rose's Kiss Review

The Ice Skating Kiss

★ ★ ★ ★

I GIVE THE ICE SKATING KISS FOUR STARS! THE PRECARIOUS FOOTING THRILLED ME WITH A SENSE OF DERRING-DO! AND FROSTY NOSES AGAINST WARM CHEEKS WILL DELIGHT ANY KISS AFICIONADO!

Rose's Kiss Review

The Kitchen Kiss

★ ★ ★ ★

PLAYFULNESS AND SURPRISE STEAL THE SHOW! A FADED BUT CLEAN LINOLEUM FLOOR AND GOLDEN OLDIES FROM A TINNY RADIO MAKE THIS KISS A TIMELESS CLASSIC! FOUR STARS!

Rose's Kiss Review

The Fireside Kiss

★ ★ ★ ★

FOUR ENTHUSIASTIC STARS FOR THE FIRESIDE KISS! HOT LIPS ARE ALWAYS INTERESTING, BUT HERE WE EXPERIENCE THEM WITH A SOUNDTRACK OF GLORIOUS SNAPS, HISSES AND CRACKLES! THE DANCING SHADOWS ARE CHOREOGRAPHIC GENIUS!

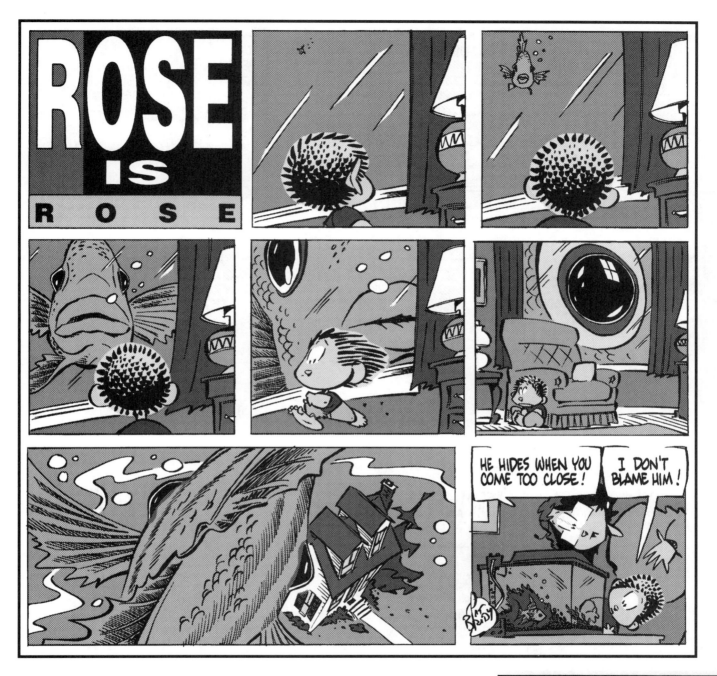

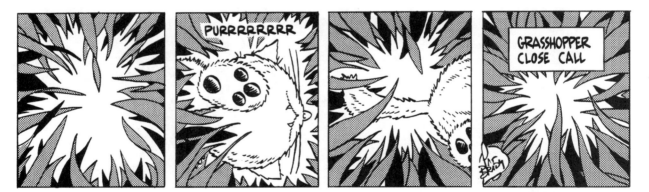

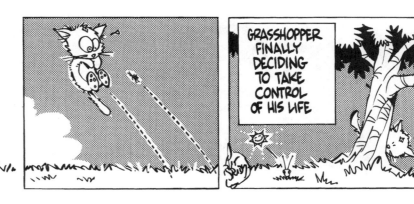

TO WATCH PASQUALE FLY PAST THE MOON, FAN THE PAGES WITH YOUR LEFT THUMB!

TO SEE PASQUALE FLY THROUGH THE ROOF, FAN THE PAGES WITH YOUR RIGHT THUMB!

43

GREAT MOMENTS IN MOVIES:
#1: THE DIMMING
OF THE THEATRE LIGHTS

GREAT MOMENTS IN MOVIES:
#2: THE SNACK BAR COMMERCIAL
COUNTING DOWN THE MINUTES
TILL SHOWTIME

45

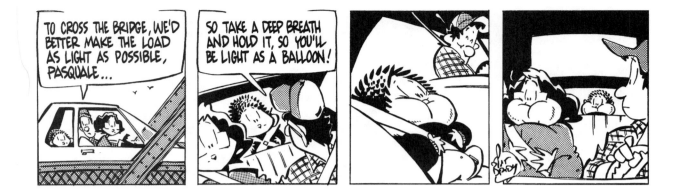

PURRR
PURRR
PURRR
PURRR
PURRR

ROARRR

ROAR

ONE FINE DAY, YOGA MASTER MAHARISHI PEEKABOO'S DISCIPLINE WAS INTERRUPTED BY A DRAGON IN THE TEMPLE...

ROAR

DURING PEACEFUL MEDITATION, YOGA MASTER MAHARISHI PEEKABOO WAS MENACED BY A DRAGON, AND LEAPED OFF A PRECIPICE TO ESCAPE.

GETTING A CLAW STUCK IN THE CLIFF'S EDGE, THE MASTER DANGLED HELPLESSLY, UNABLE TO MOVE.

ROARRR

AS THE ROARING DRAGON DREW CLOSER AND CLOSER, THE MASTER NOTICED A SOLITARY FLOWER.

ROARRR

SNIFF

HOW SWEET IT SMELLED!

ROAR

FLEEING A DRAGON, YOGA MASTER MAHARISHI PEEKABOO BECAME ENSNARED BY CATCHING A CLAW ON THE EDGE OF A CLIFF.

A WANDERING GIANT APPEARED AND SET THE MASTER FREE.

PURRR

WITH GRATITUDE, MAHARISHI PEEKABOO FOLLOWED THE GIANT UP AND DOWN THE EARTH UNTIL THE END OF TIME. AT LEAST IT SEEMED LIKE IT TO THE GIANT!

49

HOME IS WHERE THE WORLD STOPS SPINNING!

THIS INK STAMP WILL PROVE YOU PAID YOUR ADMISSION PRICE, SIR!

WELCOME TO CREATIVE PLAYLAND

ENTER

YOU'D LIKE ONE ON EACH HAND? NO PROBLEM!

AND ONE ON MY BELLY, PLEASE!

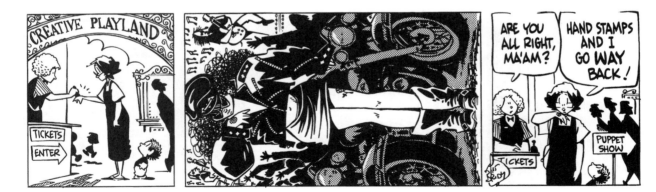

CREATIVE PLAYLAND

TICKETS
ENTER

ARE YOU ALL RIGHT, MA'AM?

HAND STAMPS AND I GO WAY BACK!

TICKETS

PUPPET SHOW

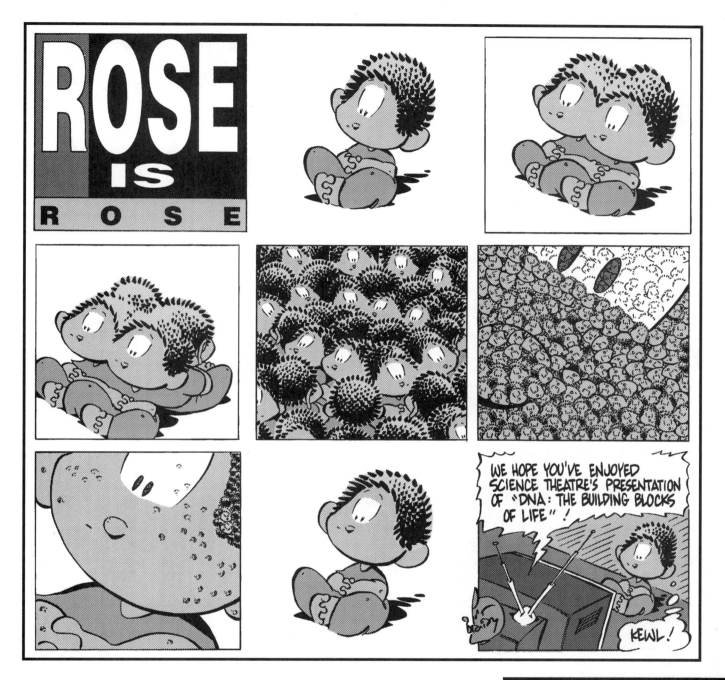

HORSERADISH SNIFF
FLASHBACK

CLICK CLICK

CLICK CLICK

THOSE LITTLE SUNS DON'T LIVE VERY LONG IN CAPTIVITY!

HUG'S-EYE VIEWS

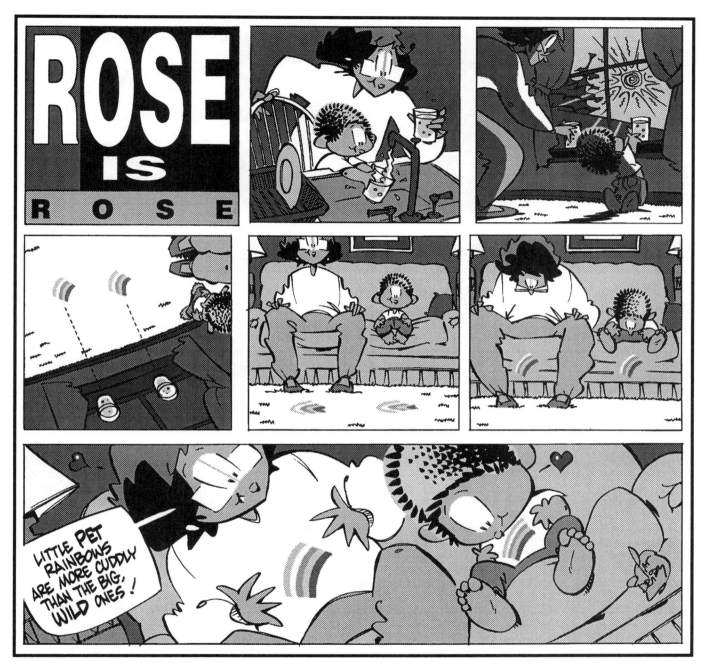

55

56

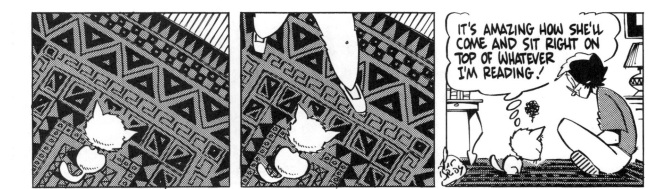

60

TO WATCH PASQUALE FLY PAST THE MOON, FAN THE PAGES WITH YOUR LEFT THUMB!

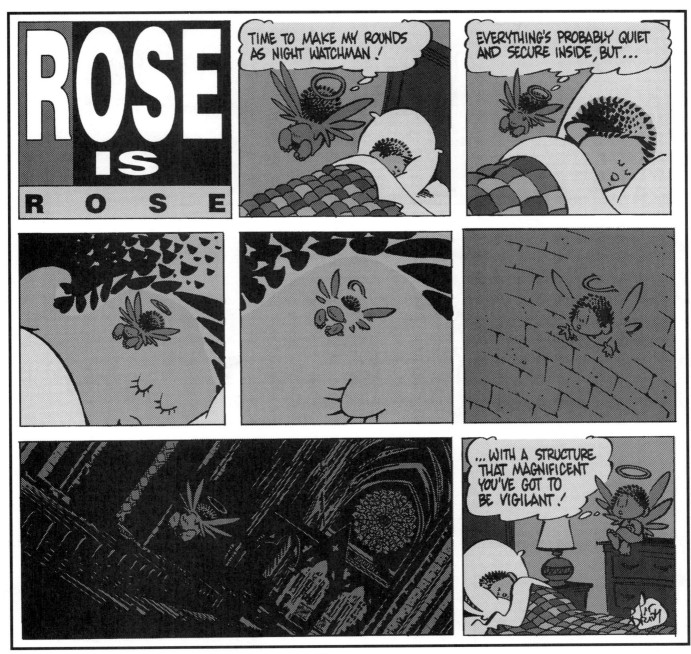

TO SEE PASQUALE FLY THROUGH THE ROOF, FAN THE PAGES WITH YOUR RIGHT THUMB!

64

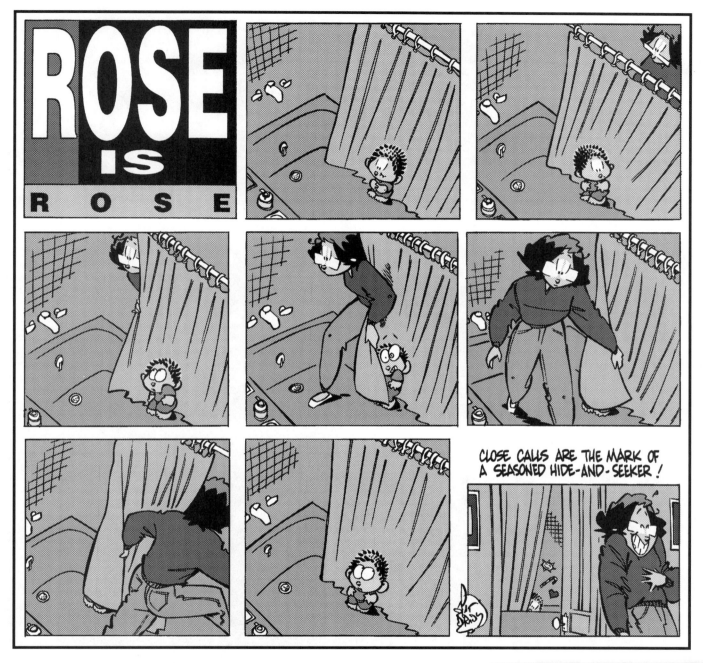

CLOSE CALLS ARE THE MARK OF
A SEASONED HIDE-AND-SEEKER!

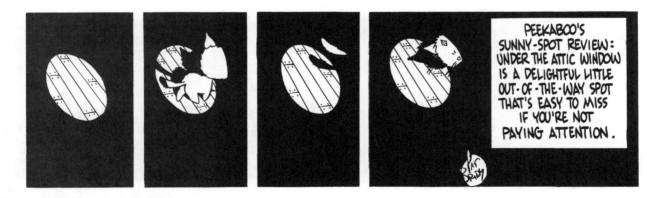

PEEKABOO'S SUNNY-SPOT REVIEW: THE SUNNY SPOT IN THE FAMILY ROOM LOOKS GREAT AND FEELS GREAT, BUT TASTES LIKE AN OLD RUG.

PEEKABOO'S SUNNY-SPOT REVIEW: UNDER THE ATTIC WINDOW IS A DELIGHTFUL LITTLE OUT-OF-THE-WAY SPOT THAT'S EASY TO MISS IF YOU'RE NOT PAYING ATTENTION.

PEEKABOO'S SUNNY-SPOT REVIEW: GETTING BACK MAY REQUIRE A CALL FOR HELP, BUT ROOFTOP SUNSHINE IS WORTH THE TROUBLE! A RISKY BUT GLORIOUS ADVENTURE, NOT FOR WUSSY PUSSIES.

PEEKABOO'S SUNNY-SPOT REVIEW: BACK TO BASICS! INSIDE OR OUTSIDE, FOR HEARTY, TRADITIONAL SUNSHINE FARE, THE WINDOW SILL IS PERFECT IN ANY SEASON. THE NO-NONSENSE NAP IS THE HOUSE SPECIALTY.

IT'S NOT EASY COMING UP WITH AN INTERESTING AND BEAUTIFUL SUNSET EVERY DAY!

SOME DAYS I STARE AT A BLANK SKY FOR HOURS WITH NO IDEAS!

AND THE DEADLINES NEVER STOP!

I'M SORRY I SAID THIS ONE WAS BORING!

NO, NO, I APPRECIATE YOUR FEEDBACK!

ANGELS **RULE** AT FACE-MAKING CONTESTS

79

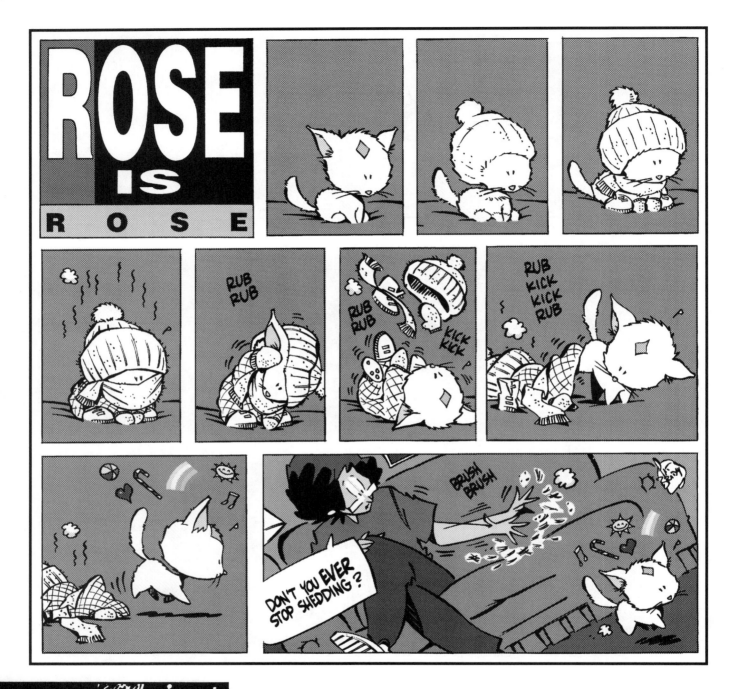

TO WATCH PASQUALE FLY PAST THE MOON, FAN THE PAGES WITH YOUR LEFT THUMB!

TO SEE PASQUALE FLY THROUGH THE ROOF, FAN THE PAGES WITH YOUR RIGHT THUMB!

DR. PEEKABOO EXAMINES A PATIENT SUFFERING FROM ANXIETY.

MEOWWWW!

THE DOCTOR RECOMMENDS AN IMMEDIATE BELLY RUB.

RUB RUB

TREATMENT IS SUCCESSFUL AND DR. PEEKABOO DENIES ANY CONFLICT OF INTEREST.

CONTINUING TREATMENT FOR ANXIETY, DR. PEEKABOO SITS ON THE PATIENT.

THE DOCTOR STIMULATES ACUPUNCTURE POINTS ON THE ABDOMEN, USING TINY, NEEDLE-LIKE CLAWS.

THE PATIENT ABRUPTLY DISCONTINUES TREATMENT, CAUSING SEVERE COMPLICATIONS.

I REALLY THINK I MAY BE **PSYCHIC**!

:GASP:

YOU WON'T BELIEVE THIS, BUT I **KNEW** YOU WERE GOING TO ROLL YOUR EYES!

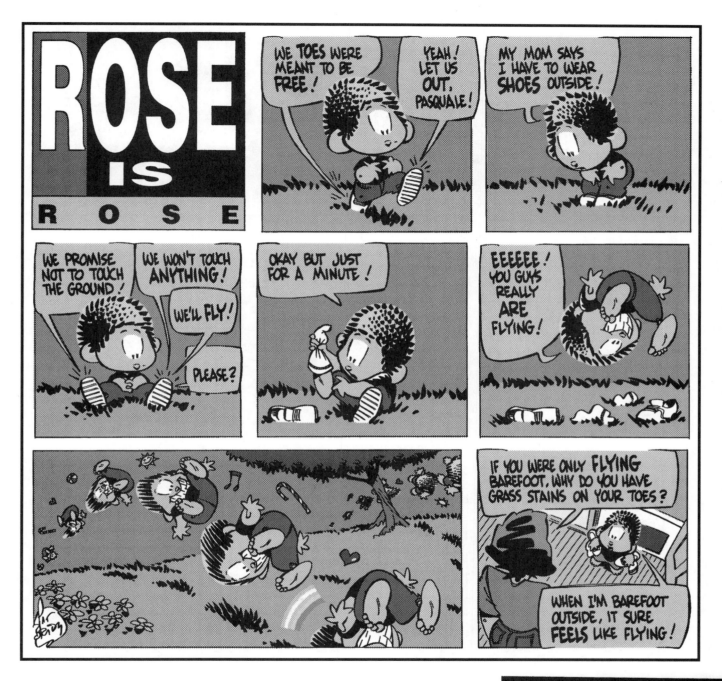

89

:CREAK:

:CREAK:

:CREAK:

:CREAK:

THERE IS NO MINIMUM AGE REQUIREMENT FOR A DREAMER'S LICENSE

I WONDER WHAT MAKES A DREAMSHIP RUN?

FUEL: USE ONLY PREMIUM WISHES

WISHES!? I'VE ALWAYS GOT A FULL TANK OF THOSE!

93

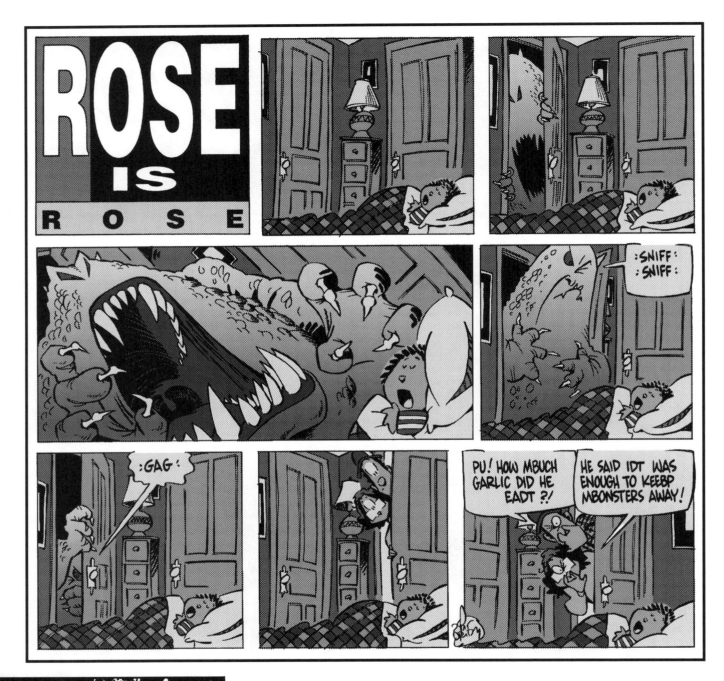

94

96

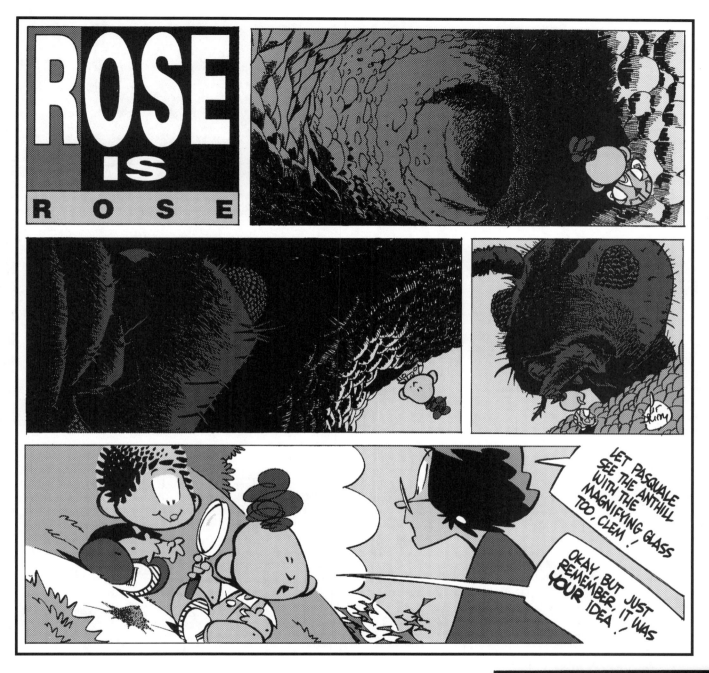

98

"CLEAN THAT UP!"

#4297
ON THE LIST OF
USELESS THINGS
TO SAY TO
A CAT

WHIRRR

EEEEEEEEEE!!

PASQUALE SUBMITTED HIS WORK TO A COPY MACHINE AND IT WAS ACCEPTED?!

HE CONSIDERS THIS HIS FIRST BIG BREAK!

I ASKED YOU TO CARRY THIS LAUNDRY WITH YOU THE NEXT TIME YOU WENT UP THE STAIRS!

SORRY, BUT I CAME UP THE BANISTER.!

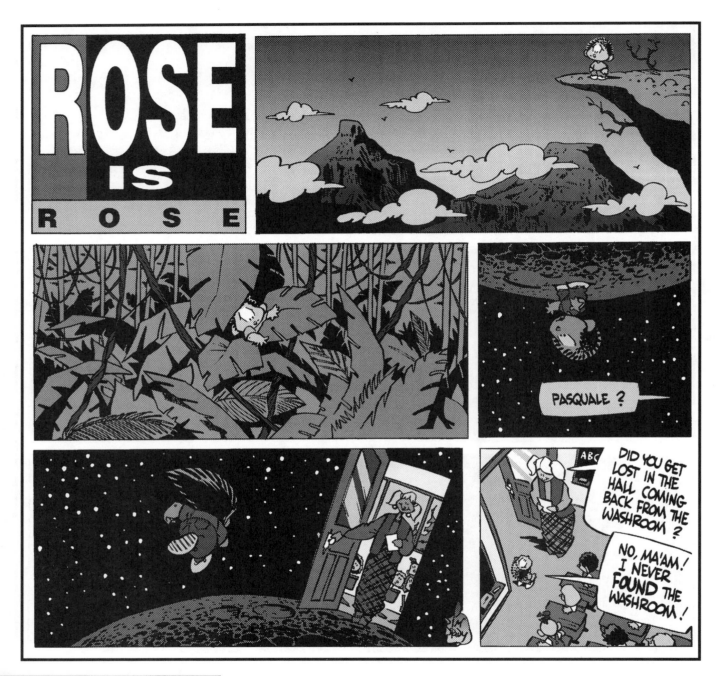

TO WATCH PASQUALE FLY PAST THE MOON, FAN THE PAGES WITH YOUR LEFT THUMB!

TO SEE PASQUALE FLY THROUGH THE ROOF, FAN THE PAGES WITH YOUR RIGHT THUMB!

103

PASQUALE'S GUARDIAN ANGEL EXAMINES THE CONTENTS OF PASQUALE'S SOUL...

THE MARILYN MONROE ARCHETYPE IS STILL UNDER CONSTRUCTION AND WON'T BE READY UNTIL I'M SURE PASQUALE IS!

PASQUALE'S GUARDIAN ANGEL EXAMINES THE CONTENTS OF PASQUALE'S SOUL...

FOR SUCH A LITTLE OUT-OF-THE-WAY SPOT, THIS IS GREAT MUSIC!

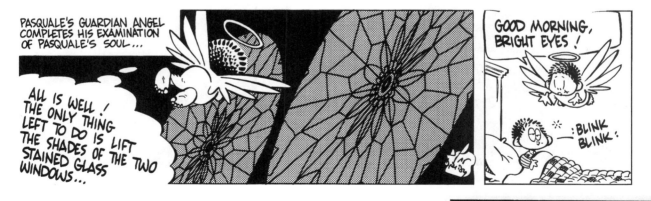

PASQUALE'S GUARDIAN ANGEL COMPLETES HIS EXAMINATION OF PASQUALE'S SOUL...

ALL IS WELL! THE ONLY THING LEFT TO DO IS LIFT THE SHADES OF THE TWO STAINED GLASS WINDOWS...

GOOD MORNING, BRIGHT EYES!

: BLINK BLINK :

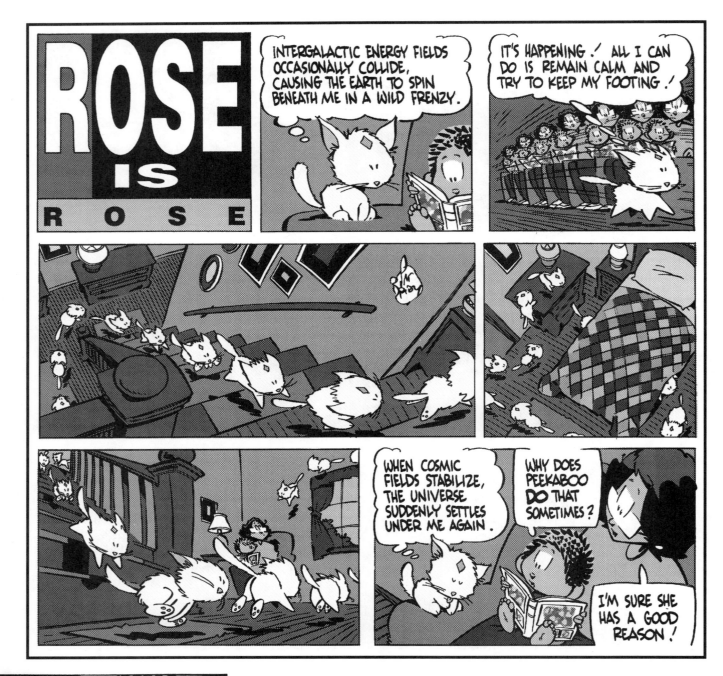

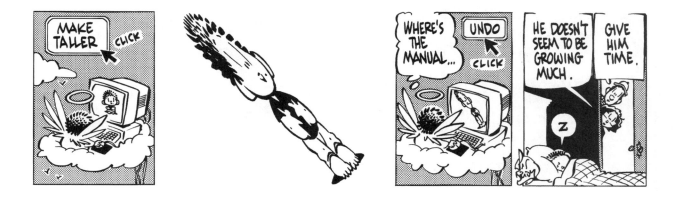

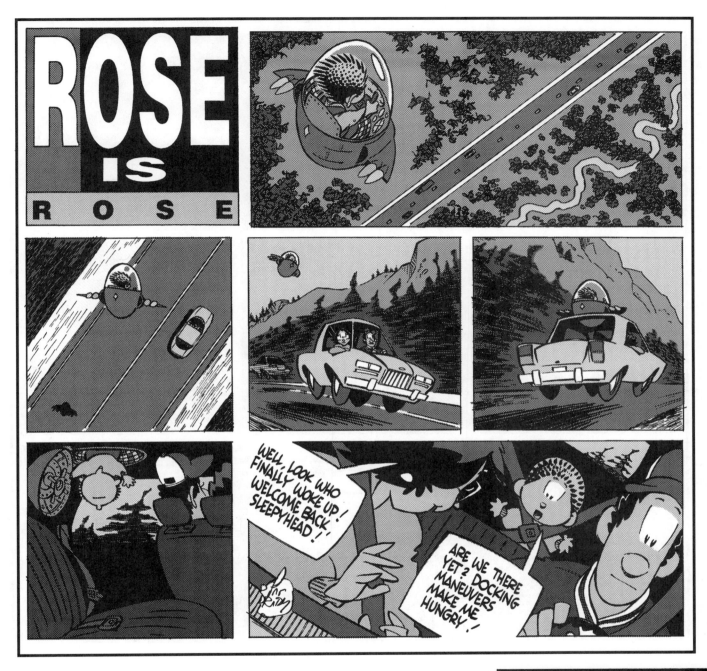

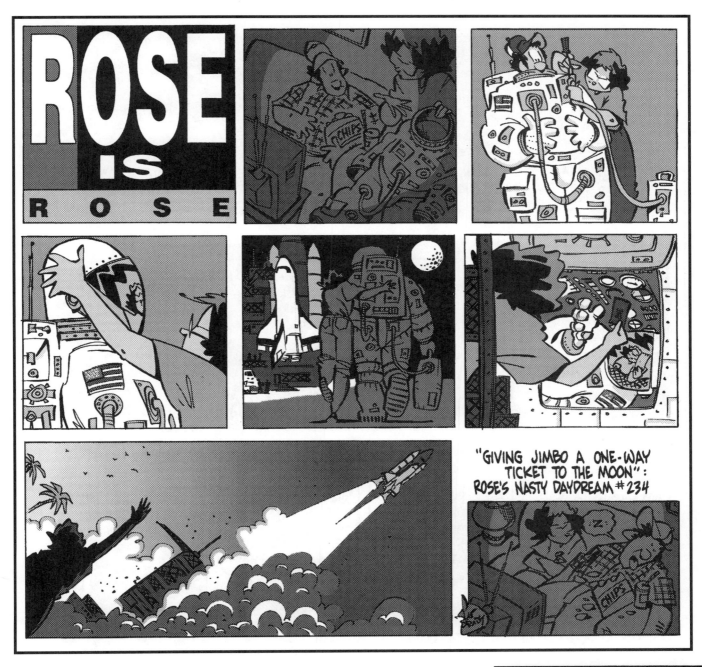

"GIVING JIMBO A ONE-WAY TICKET TO THE MOON": ROSE'S NASTY DAYDREAM #234

FIRST THEY BUILD A SHELTER AGAINST THE SUN, WIND AND RAIN...

THEN, INSIDE THE SHELTER, THEY BUILD SUN, WIND AND RAIN!

THOSE BIG, FUEL-GUZZLING BRAINS ARE *SO* INEFFICIENT!

I'VE BEEN RUNNING IN CIRCLES ALL DAY!

SO TELL ME, ROSE, ARE YOU STAYING OUT OF TROUBLE? :HAHAHA:

TEA ROOM

I'M SO FAR OUT OF TROUBLE I COULD SCREAM!

THIS KNOB ON THE SCALE TURNS *GRAVITY* UP OR DOWN!

SEE? I'VE MADE US WEIGH ONLY *ONE POUND!*

WHOA! DO YOU FEEL KIND OF *FLOATY?*

I *DO* FEEL FLOATY!

I CONCEDE THAT JIMBO'S TEASING HAS BECOME MORE GRACEFUL...

TO WATCH PASQUALE FLY PAST THE MOON, FAN THE PAGES WITH YOUR LEFT THUMB!

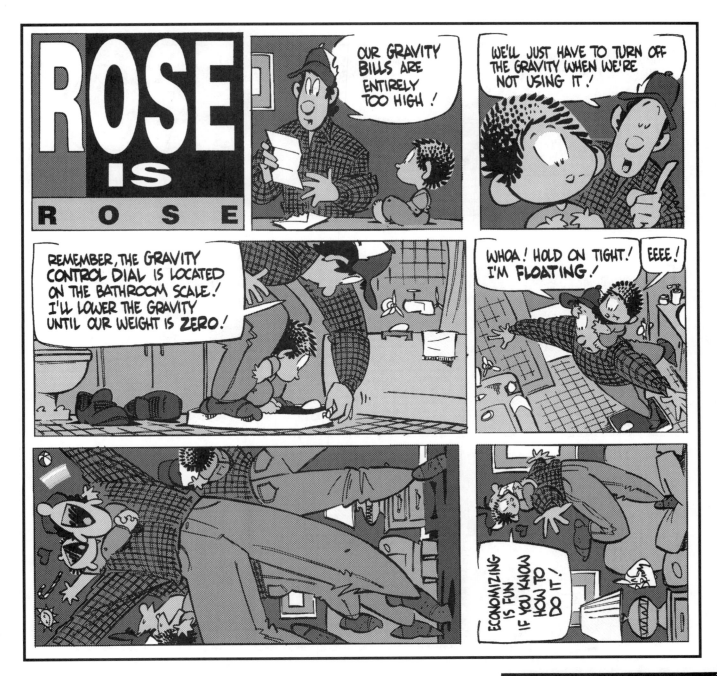

TO SEE PASQUALE FLY THROUGH THE ROOF, FAN THE PAGES WITH YOUR RIGHT THUMB!

123

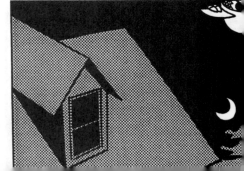